Please do not
annoy the writer.
He will put you
in a joke
and everyone will
laugh about you!

_____

_____

_____

_____

Brainstorming

Idea 1	Funny Connections	Idea 2

💡 Related topics

🐔 Puns

Characters

Joke

Setup

- -

Punchline

Brainstorming

Idea 1	Funny Connections	Idea 2

→
←

←
→

💡 Related topics

🐔 Puns

Characters

Joke

Setup

- -

Punchline

Brainstorming

Idea 1	Funny Connections	Idea 2

→
←

←
→

💡 Related topics

🐔 Puns

Characters

Joke

Setup

- -

Punchline

Brainstorming

Idea 1	Funny Connections	Idea 2

→
←

←
→

💡 Related topics

🐔 Puns

Characters

Joke

Setup

- -

Punchline

Brainstorming

Idea 1	Funny Connections	Idea 2

Related topics

Puns

Characters

Joke

Setup

Punchline

Brainstorming

Idea 1	Funny Connections	Idea 2
	→ ←	
	← →	

💡 Related topics

🐔 Puns

Characters

Joke

Setup

- -

Punchline

Brainstorming

Idea 1	Funny Connections	Idea 2

→
←

←
→

💡 Related topics

🐔 Puns

Characters

Joke

Setup

- -

Punchline

Brainstorming

Idea 1	Funny Connections	Idea 2

→
←
←
→

💡 Related topics

🐔 Puns

Characters

Joke

Setup

- -

Punchline

Brainstorming

Idea 1	Funny Connections	Idea 2

Related topics	Puns

Characters

Joke

Setup

- -

Punchline

Brainstorming

Idea 1	Funny Connections	Idea 2

Related topics

Puns

Characters

Joke

Setup

Punchline

Brainstorming

Idea 1	Funny Connections	Idea 2

💡 Related topics

🐔 Puns

Characters

Joke

Setup

- -

Punchline

Brainstorming

Idea 1	Funny Connections	Idea 2

Related topics

Puns

Characters

Joke

Setup

- -

Punchline

Brainstorming

Idea 1	Funny Connections	Idea 2

→
←
←
→

💡 Related topics

🐔 Puns

Characters

Joke

Setup

- -

Punchline

Brainstorming

Idea 1	Funny Connections	Idea 2
	→	←
	←	→

💡 Related topics

🐔 Puns

Characters

Joke

Setup

- -

Punchline

Brainstorming

Idea 1	Funny Connections	Idea 2
	→ ←	← →

💡 Related topics

🐔 Puns

Characters

Joke

Setup

- -

Punchline

Brainstorming

Idea 1	Funny Connections	Idea 2

💡 Related topics

🐔 Puns

Characters

Joke

Setup

- -

Punchline

Brainstorming

Idea 1	Funny Connections	Idea 2
	→ ←	← →

💡 Related topics

🐔 Puns

Characters

Joke

Setup

- -

Punchline

Brainstorming

Idea 1	Funny Connections	Idea 2

Related topics

Puns

Characters

Joke

Setup

- -

Punchline

Brainstorming

Idea 1	Funny Connections	Idea 2

Related topics

Puns

Characters

Joke

Setup

- -

Punchline

Brainstorming

Idea 1	Funny Connections	Idea 2

Related topics

Puns

Characters

Joke

Setup

- -

Punchline

Brainstorming

Idea 1	Funny Connections	Idea 2

Related topics

Puns

Characters

Joke

Setup

- -

Punchline

Brainstorming

Idea 1	Funny Connections	Idea 2
	→ ←	
	⇄ ⇄	

💡 Related topics

🐔 Puns

Characters

Joke

Setup

- -

Punchline

Brainstorming

Idea 1	Funny Connections	Idea 2

→
←

←
→

💡 Related topics

🐔 Puns

Characters

Joke

Setup

- -

Punchline

Brainstorming

Idea 1	Funny Connections	Idea 2

Related topics

Puns

Characters

Joke

Setup

- -

Punchline

Brainstorming

Idea 1	Funny Connections	Idea 2
	→ ←	← →

💡 Related topics

🐔 Puns

Characters

Joke

Setup

- -

Punchline

Brainstorming

Idea 1	Funny Connections	Idea 2

Related topics

Puns

Characters

Joke

Setup

Punchline

Brainstorming

Idea 1	Funny Connections	Idea 2
	→ ←	← →

💡 Related topics

🐔 Puns

Characters

Joke

Setup

- -

Punchline

Brainstorming

Idea 1	Funny Connections	Idea 2

Related topics

Puns

Characters

Joke

Setup

- -

Punchline

Brainstorming

Idea 1	Funny Connections	Idea 2
	→ ← ← →	

💡 Related topics

🐔 Puns

Characters

Joke

Setup

- -

Punchline

Brainstorming

Idea 1	Funny Connections	Idea 2

Related topics

Puns

Characters

Joke

Setup

- -

Punchline

Brainstorming

Idea 1	Funny Connections	Idea 2

Related topics

Puns

Characters

Joke

Setup

Punchline

Brainstorming

Idea 1	Funny Connections	Idea 2
	→ ←	← →

💡 Related topics

🐔 Puns

Characters

Joke

Setup

- -

Punchline

Brainstorming

Idea 1	Funny Connections	Idea 2

Related topics

Puns

Characters

Joke

Setup

- -

Punchline

Brainstorming

Idea 1	Funny Connections	Idea 2

Related topics

Puns

Characters

Joke

Setup

Punchline

Brainstorming

Idea 1	Funny Connections	Idea 2

💡 Related topics

🐔 Puns

Characters

Joke

Setup

- -

Punchline

Brainstorming

Idea 1	Funny Connections	Idea 2

→
←

←
→

💡 Related topics

🐔 Puns

Characters

Joke

Setup

- -

Punchline

Brainstorming

Idea 1	Funny Connections	Idea 2

Related topics

Puns

Characters

Joke

Setup

Punchline

Brainstorming

Idea 1	Funny Connections	Idea 2

Related topics

Puns

Characters

Joke

Setup

Punchline

Brainstorming

Idea 1	Funny Connections	Idea 2

💡 Related topics

🐔 Puns

Characters

Joke

Setup

- -

Punchline

Brainstorming

Idea 1	Funny Connections	Idea 2

→
←

←
→

💡 Related topics

🐔 Puns

Characters

Joke

Setup

- -

Punchline

Brainstorming

Idea 1	Funny Connections	Idea 2

Related topics

Puns

Characters

Joke

Setup

Punchline

Brainstorming

Idea 1	Funny Connections	Idea 2
	→ ← ← →	

💡 Related topics

🐔 Puns

Characters

Joke

Setup

- -

Punchline

Brainstorming

Idea 1	Funny Connections	Idea 2

💡 Related topics

🐔 Puns

Characters

Joke

Setup

Punchline

Brainstorming

Idea 1	Funny Connections	Idea 2

→
←

←
→

💡 Related topics

🐔 Puns

Characters

Joke

Setup

- -

Punchline

Brainstorming

Idea 1	Funny Connections	Idea 2

Related topics

Puns

Characters

Joke

Setup

Punchline

Brainstorming

Idea 1	Funny Connections	Idea 2

💡 Related topics

🐔 Puns

Characters

Joke

Setup

Punchline

Brainstorming

Idea 1	Funny Connections	Idea 2

→
←

←
→

💡 Related topics

🐔 Puns

Characters

Joke

Setup

- -

Punchline

Brainstorming

Idea 1	Funny Connections	Idea 2

→
←

←
→

💡 Related topics

🐔 Puns

Characters

Joke

Setup

- -

Punchline

Brainstorming

Idea 1	Funny Connections	Idea 2
	→ ⇄ ←	

💡 Related topics

🐔 Puns

Characters

Joke

Setup

- -

Punchline

Brainstorming

Idea 1	Funny Connections	Idea 2
	→ ←	
	← →	

💡 Related topics

🐔 Puns

Characters

Joke

Setup

- -

Punchline

Brainstorming

Idea 1	Funny Connections	Idea 2

→
←

←
→

💡 Related topics

🐔 Puns

Characters

Joke

Setup

Punchline

Brainstorming

Idea 1	Funny Connections	Idea 2

Related topics

Puns

Characters

Joke

Setup

Punchline

Brainstorming

Idea 1	Funny Connections	Idea 2

Related topics

Puns

Characters

Joke

Setup

Punchline

Brainstorming

Idea 1	Funny Connections	Idea 2

Related topics

Puns

Characters

Joke

Setup

Punchline

Brainstorming

Idea 1	Funny Connections	Idea 2

💡 Related topics

🐔 Puns

Characters

Joke

Setup

- -

Punchline

Brainstorming

Idea 1	Funny Connections	Idea 2

Related topics

Puns

Characters

Joke

Setup

- -

Punchline

Brainstorming

Idea 1	Funny Connections	Idea 2

→
←

←
→

💡 Related topics

🐔 Puns

Characters

Joke

Setup

- -

Punchline

Brainstorming

Idea 1	Funny Connections	Idea 2

💡 Related topics

🐔 Puns

Characters

Joke

Setup

Punchline

Brainstorming

Idea 1	Funny Connections	Idea 2

→
⇄ ←

← →

💡 Related topics

🐔 Puns

Characters

Joke

Setup

- -

Punchline

Brainstorming

Idea 1	Funny Connections	Idea 2

→
⇄
←
→

💡 Related topics

🐔 Puns

Characters

Joke

Setup

- -

Punchline

Brainstorming

Idea 1	Funny Connections	Idea 2
	→ ←	
	← →	

💡 Related topics

🐔 Puns

Characters

Joke

Setup

- -

Punchline

Brainstorming

Idea 1	Funny Connections	Idea 2

💡 Related topics

🐔 Puns

Characters

Joke

Setup

Punchline

Brainstorming

Idea 1	Funny Connections	Idea 2

💡 Related topics

🐔 Puns

Characters

Joke

Setup

Punchline

Brainstorming

Idea 1	Funny Connections	Idea 2

Related topics

Puns

Characters

Joke

Setup

Punchline

Brainstorming

Idea 1	Funny Connections	Idea 2

→
←
←
→

💡 Related topics

🐔 Puns

Characters

Joke

Setup

- -

Punchline

Brainstorming

Idea 1	Funny Connections	Idea 2

→
←

←
→

💡 Related topics

🐔 Puns

Characters

Joke

Setup

- -

Punchline

Brainstorming

Idea 1	Funny Connections	Idea 2

Related topics

Puns

Characters

Joke

Setup

Punchline

Brainstorming

Idea 1	Funny Connections	Idea 2

💡 Related topics

🐔 Puns

Characters

Joke

Setup

- -

Punchline

Brainstorming

Idea 1	Funny Connections	Idea 2
	→ ⇆ ←	
	← ⇆ →	

💡 Related topics

🐔 Puns

Characters

Joke

Setup

- -

Punchline

Brainstorming

Idea 1	Funny Connections	Idea 2

💡 Related topics

🐔 Puns

Characters

Joke

Setup

- -

Punchline

Brainstorming

Idea 1	Funny Connections	Idea 2

→
←
←
→

💡 Related topics

🐔 Puns

Characters

Joke

Setup

- -

Punchline

Brainstorming

Idea 1	Funny Connections	Idea 2

💡 Related topics

🐔 Puns

Characters

Joke

Setup

Punchline

Brainstorming

Idea 1	Funny Connections	Idea 2
	→ ← ← →	

💡 Related topics

🐔 Puns

Characters

Joke

Setup

- -

Punchline

Brainstorming

Idea 1	Funny Connections	Idea 2
	→ ← ← →	

💡 Related topics

🐔 Puns

Characters

Joke

Setup

- -

Punchline

Brainstorming

Idea 1	Funny Connections	Idea 2

Related topics

Puns

Characters

Joke

Setup

Punchline

Brainstorming

Idea 1	Funny Connections	Idea 2

→
←
←
→

💡 Related topics

🐔 Puns

Characters

Joke

Setup

- -

Punchline

Brainstorming

Idea 1	Funny Connections	Idea 2

Related topics	Puns

Characters

Joke

Setup

Punchline

Brainstorming

Idea 1	Funny Connections	Idea 2

Related topics

Puns

Characters

Joke

Setup

Punchline

Brainstorming

Idea 1	Funny Connections	Idea 2

💡 Related topics

🐔 Puns

Characters

Joke

Setup

- -

Punchline

Brainstorming

Idea 1	Funny Connections	Idea 2

💡 Related topics

🐔 Puns

Characters

Joke

Setup

- -

Punchline

Brainstorming

Idea 1	Funny Connections	Idea 2

Related topics

Puns

Characters

Joke

Setup

Punchline

Brainstorming

Idea 1	Funny Connections	Idea 2
	→ ←	← →

💡 Related topics

🐔 Puns

Characters

Joke

Setup

Punchline

Brainstorming

Idea 1	Funny Connections	Idea 2

Related topics

Puns

Characters

Joke

Setup

Punchline

Brainstorming

Idea 1	Funny Connections	Idea 2

Related topics

Puns

Characters

Joke

Setup

- -

Punchline

Brainstorming

Idea 1	Funny Connections	Idea 2

Related topics	Puns

Characters

Joke

Setup

Punchline

Brainstorming

Idea 1	Funny Connections	Idea 2

Related topics

Puns

Characters

Joke

Setup

Punchline

Brainstorming

Idea 1	Funny Connections	Idea 2

Related topics

Puns

Characters

Joke

Setup

- -

Punchline

Brainstorming

Idea 1	Funny Connections	Idea 2

Related topics

Puns

Characters

Joke

Setup

Punchline

Brainstorming

Idea 1	Funny Connections	Idea 2

→
←
←
→

💡 Related topics

🐔 Puns

Characters

Joke

Setup

- -

Punchline

Brainstorming

Idea 1	Funny Connections	Idea 2
	→ ←	
	← →	

💡 Related topics

🐔 Puns

Characters

Joke

Setup

- - - - - - - - - - - - - - - - - - - -

Punchline

Brainstorming

Idea 1	Funny Connections	Idea 2

💡 Related topics

🐔 Puns

Characters

Joke

Setup

- -

Punchline

Brainstorming

Idea 1	Funny Connections	Idea 2

Related topics

Puns

Characters

Joke

Setup

Punchline

Brainstorming

Idea 1	Funny Connections	Idea 2

→
←

←
→

💡 Related topics

🐔 Puns

Characters

Joke

Setup

- -

Punchline

Brainstorming

Idea 1	Funny Connections	Idea 2

Related topics

Puns

Characters

Joke

Setup

Punchline

Brainstorming

Idea 1	Funny Connections	Idea 2

💡 Related topics

🐓 Puns

Characters

Joke

Setup

- -

Punchline

Brainstorming

Idea 1	Funny Connections	Idea 2

→
←

←
→

💡 Related topics

🐔 Puns

Characters

Joke

Setup

- -

Punchline

Brainstorming

Idea 1	Funny Connections	Idea 2
	→ ←	
	⇄ ⇄	

💡 Related topics

🐓 Puns

Characters

Joke

Setup

- - - - - - - - - - - - - - - - - - - -

Punchline

Brainstorming

Idea 1	Funny Connections	Idea 2

→
←

←
→

💡 Related topics

🐔 Puns

Characters

Joke

Setup

- -

Punchline

Brainstorming

Idea 1	Funny Connections	Idea 2

💡 Related topics

🐔 Puns

Characters

Joke

Setup

Punchline

Brainstorming

Idea 1	Funny Connections	Idea 2

Related topics

Puns

Characters

Joke

Setup

Punchline

Brainstorming

Idea 1	Funny Connections	Idea 2

💡 Related topics

🐔 Puns

Characters

Joke

Setup

Punchline

Brainstorming

Idea 1	Funny Connections	Idea 2

Related topics

Puns

Characters

Joke

Setup

Punchline

Brainstorming

Idea 1	Funny Connections	Idea 2
	→ ←	← →

💡 Related topics

🐔 Puns

Characters

Joke

Setup

- -

Punchline

Brainstorming

Idea 1	Funny Connections	Idea 2
	→ ⇄ ←	← ⇄ →

💡 Related topics

🐔 Puns

Characters

Joke

Setup

- -

Punchline

Brainstorming

Idea 1	Funny Connections	Idea 2

→
←

←
→

💡 Related topics

🐔 Puns

Characters

Joke

Setup

- -

Punchline

Brainstorming

Idea 1	Funny Connections	Idea 2

Related topics

Puns

Characters

Joke

Setup

Punchline

Brainstorming

Idea 1	Funny Connections	Idea 2

Related topics

Puns

Characters

Joke

Setup

- -

Punchline

Brainstorming

Idea 1	Funny Connections	Idea 2

→
←

←
→

💡 Related topics

🐔 Puns

Characters

Joke

Setup

- -

Punchline

36534622R00063